T0196582

# POETIC
## HEART-TO-HEART
*Messages*

## MARTHA J. BUTLER

# POETIC HEART-TO-HEART MESSAGES

*Copyright © 2015 Martha J. Butler.*

*All rights reserved. No part of this book may be used or reproduced by any means, graphic, electronic, or mechanical, including photocopying, recording, taping or by any information storage retrieval system without the written permission of the author except in the case of brief quotations embodied in critical articles and reviews.*

*iUniverse books may be ordered through booksellers or by contacting:*

*iUniverse*
*1663 Liberty Drive*
*Bloomington, IN 47403*
*www.iuniverse.com*
*1-800-Authors (1-800-288-4677)*

*Because of the dynamic nature of the Internet, any web addresses or links contained in this book may have changed since publication and may no longer be valid. The views expressed in this work are solely those of the author and do not necessarily reflect the views of the publisher, and the publisher hereby disclaims any responsibility for them.*

*Any people depicted in stock imagery provided by Thinkstock are models,*
*and such images are being used for illustrative purposes only.*
*Certain stock imagery © Thinkstock.*

*ISBN: 978-1-5320-3149-6 (sc)*
*ISBN: 978-1-5320-3148-9 (e)*

*Library of Congress Control Number: 2017916555*

*Print information available on the last page.*

*iUniverse rev. date: 10/30/2017*

# Stay Positive

A battery has two symbols: + for positive and – for negative.

The symbols represent strength and weakness.

A battery needs to be strong all the time.

A weak battery is negative, maybe dead.

Consider yourself a powerful battery.

Make sure your thoughts are always positive.

Keep a positive mental attitude.

Get rid of criticism and doubt.

Believe in yourself.

Be a strong battery with a positive charge.

Live each day as a rechargeable battery.

Charge your battery often.

Do not become a dead battery.

Where is your charging station?

Your charging station is in your family,

Your thoughts, your friends, and other positive people.

When you find yourself weak, picking up negative energy,

Physically and mentally get on the move.

Go to a positive place by changing your position.

Transform your thoughts from weak to strong.

You have control over how you feel.

Practice being a positive force every day.

May the force of your strength stay with you.

# The Fabric That Binds

Mother, father, sister, and brother—
Love is the fabric that binds.
We are bound by the same fabric.
No matter how hard we try to forget,
Love is always there—in your heart.
We fool ourselves into believing
Love no longer exists, yet it still lives.
God is love inside each of us,
Always a part of us.
Denial is what keeps us apart.
Then the day arrives when we
Come face-to-face with the truth,
The shoulda, coulda, woulda truth—
The day you regret not having
Reached out and touched your mother
Father, sister, or brother,
Regret that will follow you always,
Knowing precious time was lost
That will never be shared because
It is too late to forgive and reunite,
Too late to say, "I am sorry."
God has wrapped your loved one in His
Loving arms to hold forever.

# In Between

In between today and tomorrow,
Love and forgiveness,
Yesterday and today;
In between remembering and forgetting,
The past and the present;
In between
Joy and happiness—
In between all is forgiveness.
Forgiveness is the bridge
To living a fulfilling life.
Build your bridge of forgiveness.
Do not live in between.
Embrace life, and live for today.

# When the Lights Come On

When the lights come on,
Will you be clothed or naked?
Will you be ready or afraid?
To look at yourself in the mirror,
The mirror of life
Shows who you are deep inside,
The person inside your heart,
Ready to stand tall in your convictions,
Ready to accept your true reflection.
When the lights come on,
It will be the time to see your true self.
You cannot hide when the lights come on.
Will you be clothed in your true self?
Or, will you be revealed in your nakedness?
You will see for yourself who you really are
When the lights come on.
Only you will face the truth.
Don't be afraid—be ready
To face the real person
Whom you see in your mirror of life.
The power to be proud is yours
When the lights come on.

# *Message to a Daughter*

She gave you life; she gave you joy.
She gave you happiness; she gave you love.
She brought you up and cared for you,
Giving you all of herself, making you strong,
Giving you the best part of her,
Her never-ending love never giving up on you.
She released you into the world.
And the world gave to you too.
From this world, you awakened
To the adventure it provided,
To the ecstasy and the fantasy.
You were touched by the joy of discovery.
You were lulled into the excitement of being.
You have faced the harsh reality of being grown-up.
You have become a woman in your own right.
I believe in your heart of hearts you know.
It is time to let her back into your life.
I ask you to release your fear, worry, and doubt.
I ask you to remember who she really is.
Remember the days you had soup together.
Remember the joy of that warm bowl of soup.
Time waits for no one, and time is running out.
She needs the comfort of your loving arms.
The time is now. Come back to her.

# *Twilight*

*Twilight is where I am. Where are you?*
*In these days of decline, more endings than beginnings,*
*This is the time in my life when reflections are clearer*
*And I think of you. I miss you.*
*I have been waiting here for you a long time.*
*I know I won't be here many more years.*
*This is my twilight—when the lights dim and darkness begins,*
*One day, I will close my eyes and sleep peacefully.*
*Come to me, won't you, in this, my twilight?*
*While I can hold you and share these precious few years,*
*We don't know the day nor the hour when the darkness will take over*
*When we will run out of time to hold each other.*
*So now in my twilight, know that I love you with my whole heart.*
*Come to me in this time before the lights go out on us. Come.*

# What Are You Thinking?

I often wonder what you are thinking.
I wonder what is holding you back.
What are the fears that bind and keep you away?
I wonder if you realize your own power
To release the thoughts that bind.
You have the power to take the road less traveled,
The road that will bring back our joy and smiles,
The road of forgiveness and love.
Are you thinking about what the right time is to return?
I wonder if you are coming back tomorrow.
Do not be afraid; love waits for you.
Think of the power you have—you are powerful.
Think of the joy you hold, and come to me.
God forgives, I forgive, and you can forgive.
What are you thinking right now?

# *Today*

*The joy of today is in my heart.*
*Today, I choose to wait for your love*
*In my heart, in my mind.*
*Today, I choose to feel joy.*
*You are a part of my journey.*
*You remain in my heart even though*
*You are absent from my life.*
*We need each other.*
*We are special people who need each other.*
*Just to hold your hand for a minute, a second,*
*To see your smile brings reassurance of the love in this world*
*And that someone quietly knows you are needed.*
*We are special people who can choose to talk together.*
*Come to me, child—let us reconnect and talk.*

# These Are My Last Good Years

Do you know these are my last good years—
My last years to yearn and hope for your return?
It is not difficult to say because I know.
I know our days are numbered, yet I wait.
As I count the days and the years that have passed,
My heart tells me these are the last years.
My weary heart, my heavy heart, reviews our past
In wonderment of what harm I could have done
To cause such a riff that came between our loves—
The bond of trust and unconditional love,
The love a mother will always hold in her heart,
The love that keeps me waiting for your return,
The unconditional love that is yours to reclaim.
The time is now that you return to me, because
These are my last good years.

# You Are the Light

*You are the light; I gave you life.*
*Let your light shine on me.*
*Come to me, and love me again.*
*Love me the way you loved me as a child,*
*Before you knew the ways of the world.*
*Where is my sweet and wonderful child?*
*I know where she is—she is hiding inside,*
*Inside the person you have grown to be.*
*She is still there, afraid to come to me.*
*What fear is so strong that it keeps you away from me?*
*What force is it that holds your heart for the world but not for me?*
*You are the light that leads to the end of the rainbow,*
*The source of inspiration and strength,*
*The rock that anchors, and the spirit that guides.*
*You are the love that I need to pull me out of the darkness.*
*The darkness will leave; light and senses will reappear*
*When you return to me in joy to be by my side.*
*You are the light; I gave you life.*

# Remember How Much You Loved Me

Do you remember the time we shared
When life was good and sweet,
The tender times of joy and smiles
When we would always meet?
I remember all the joys,
All the days of smiles and hugs.
I remember the good times we had.
I remember with a mind full of wonder.
My heart remembers, and I can't forget
My sweet daughter of early years.
No matter the time or events,
I wait for her return—I wait for her smile,
The smile that has been lost for so long.
I know and I believe it is hiding, just waiting.
I feel the time is coming; I pray it will not be
Too late for me to see and feel the joy.
My heart longs to see her smile—I wait.

# *Time Is a Healer*

*Healing is happening every day,*
*But for me, this is my darkest hour.*
*Every day you are not present in my life,*
*Time is the enemy when I wake up in the morning,*
*When I am wandering through my day*
*Missing you, missing my sweet grandsons.*
*Time is the blade that cuts into my heart*
*And, piece by piece, destroys my hope with scars—*
*The hope I hold that someday my arms*
*Will hold you again … your arms will hold me again;*
*That one day, I will be in the arms of my grandsons.*
*Time is not a healer for me today.*
*Time is darkness every day I am without you,*
*Darkness without my grandsons whom I love*
*More than words can say.*
*I carry on looking forward to the day that*
*Time will stop when the three of you will*
*Stand before me, arms open wide,*
*Welcoming me back into your life.*
*That day—that hour, that moment, that second—*
*Time will become my healer, and*
*The scars of loneliness will disappear;*
*They will disappear instantaneously.*
*Then and only then, time will become my healer.*
*Time will then heal my heart of the darkness that has*
*Surrounded me for the many years you have been gone.*
*It's time for you to come back to me before it is too late.*
*It is time for time to be my healer.*

# Looking Down on Me

I planted a seed and asked God to make sure it would grow.
The seed was my prayer you would come to me.
That was the last seed I planted, and now you are here with me.
Today, my eyes are closed, and you stand looking down on me.
Know in your heart that I prayed for the day you would return to me.
On this day, my prayers have been answered.
All the days I prayed for your return have come to rest on this day—
This day when my eyes are closed and you are looking down on me.
My prayers are answered. God works in His own time.
You waited, and my time ran out; now, you are looking down on me.
You are here, and I thank God. I loved you with all my heart.

# *Second Chances*

*Every moment in life is a second chance,*
*A chance to celebrate today.*
*The past is your ally in repairing your present.*
*Let's get together to ensure a better future—*
*A better future for you and for me,*
*A better future for my grandchildren,*
*A happier time for us because we have missed so much.*
*I need a second chance to be whole—*
*Another chance for forgiveness and joy.*
*This moment is the moment for a second chance.*

# Never Hide

Never be who you are not.
Never change who you are.
Never just go quietly,
Because true individuals
Never hide.

# *Sunshine*

*As sure as the sun shines tomorrow,*
*I will wake up and find joy.*
*Joy in the morning is what I long for.*
*Have I forgotten about feeling the joy?*
*Sunshine will bring me happiness,*
*Erasing the sorrow of yesterday.*
*I will wake up and breathe in fresh, clean air,*
*Awaking to a new day—a gift from God,*
*A day that I will embrace and discover the joy,*
*The joy I have overlooked for so long.*
*I did not look for the blessings of today.*
*I looked back at the blessings of yesterday.*
*Joy comes with finding the blessings of this day.*
*Today, I will choose to find joy—*
*The joy that has been here all the time,*
*The joy sunshine brings when I open the blinds,*
*Embracing the sunshine with a brand-new chance for joy.*

# Invisible Walls

*There are walls all around.*
*They were built year by year.*
*I was never able to see them—you could.*
*You saw them as they were being built.*
*They are invisible because you created them.*
*You saw them in every childhood disappointment.*
*You saw them in every reprimand.*
*You saw them in every painful parental restraint.*
*The walls were built by the love of protection,*
*The protection of motherly love.*
*These invisible walls can be torn down.*
*You alone have the power to remove them.*
*I am waiting for you to break through them.*
*Stop standing on the other side of the walls—*
*Walls that have kept us apart for so long.*
*Invisible walls cannot bear the weight of a forgiving heart.*
*The time has come for you to open your heart.*
*Remove the walls one breath at a time; forgive, and come to me.*

# A New Heart

*My heart has been broken for a long time.*
*It is time for a new heart.*
*I will use the words of God and create a new heart—*
*A new heart full of goodness and joy;*
*A new heart to lift and make me soar;*
*A new heart that cares and is filled with love,*
*Leaving behind the pain of the past;*
*A new heart full of happiness;*
*A heart without pain, full of forgiveness;*
*A kind new heart getting a new start,*
*New and strong, feeling righteous,*
*Choosing to believe that now is the*
*Time for joy and renewal.*
*The time is now for a new and joyful heart.*

# The Battle

There is a battle for us to fight.
As children, we find our power.
We fight the battle of shyness and overcome.
The struggle takes time, and we win.
We fight the battle against aging and compromise.
The battle with illness is an ongoing struggle.
Sometimes, the fight is fierce and unforgiving.
We become engaged in winning and fight harder.
The battle of wills is a battle of probability.
Will you come to me today or tomorrow?
If you do not give in and come to me, this battle will
Continue to rage, and you will burn out.
As you fight the battle to love or not to love,
You are fighting a losing battle, and when I am gone,
My battle will be over, and a new battle will begin for you.
Regret will fill your heart that you did not come to me.
You will fight the battle of regret every day.
The first year will be the hardest each passing day,
Each special occasion, and in quiet moments.
You recognize your fight with the battle of regret
Will keep you fighting forever.

# *Soup*

Soup is waiting for us.
Let's have soup together,
Just like old times in days past.
I remember the time we shared soup.
I can taste that warm, good soup.
I can see you as you enjoy each spoonful.
The memory of our soup days lingers in my heart.
I would love to have soup with you today.
Come over, and let's have soup.
Any day is good for soup—just you and me.
Soup is waiting, and I am waiting for you
To get together with me and have soup.
We can celebrate today and look to tomorrow.
Oh, that wonderful soup—it smells so good.

# *Finding Myself*

*In the space between my thoughts,*
*Finding the time to be alone*
*With myself, I find myself.*
*Who am I? This mysterious person;*
*This loving, caring person;*
*This fearful person*
*Who loves life and feels that*
*Everything is right within—*
*What does she want?*
*What does she need?*
*She needs to know who she is*
*And what she wants.*
*Finding herself in a maze of success,*
*Finding herself in a maze of perception,*
*What is real in her life or not real?*
*Finding herself in the spaces*
*Between her thoughts,*
*One day, she will be whole*
*When she finds herself*
*In the beautiful person*
*She already is,*
*Sweet spaces between her thoughts.*

# Daughter

*You are the daughter your mother holds dearly*
*In her heart, and she is waiting.*
*She does not know what else to do except wait.*
*She waits in fear that you will wait too long, and*
*She may not be here when you are ready.*
*The time is now to put an end to this waiting.*
*Put an end to her yearning for your return.*
*Put an end to her pain in not having the arms*
*Of her grandchildren to embrace her.*
*She wants more than anything to feel the arms*
*Of her grandsons, whom she has missed so much.*
*Don't you miss your mother*
*Just enough to come and say, "We love you,"*
*To give her what money cannot buy—your love?*
*Just know she will wait forever for the three of you.*

# Discontent

*Feelings of listlessness,*
*Empty and lost,*
*Lost in this world of opportunity,*
*Underprivileged in a world of plenty—*
*Why so ungrateful?*
*Why so sad?*
*What will tomorrow bring—*
*A ray of light,*
*A ray of hope,*
*A sense of self?*
*Will I be strong?*
*Will I find my way?*
*Clarity is what I need.*
*Purpose is my heart's desire.*
*So lost, I cry.*
*Still, I must go on.*

# *Chains*

*There are chains all around you.*
*Who put these chains around you?*
*They seem to get tighter with time.*
*Where did they come from?*
*They came from within.*
*These chains hold on tight.*
*They hold your fear, your doubt.*
*They hold negativity and anger.*
*Only you can allow the chains to hold you.*
*The time has come for you to remove them.*
*You must begin to remove the sadness and doubt.*
*Rid yourself of negative thoughts.*
*Let go of fear; let go of doubt.*
*One by one, break each link, and*
*Free yourself so you can live again.*
*It's your time to be free.*

# Come to Me

There is joy in my life today.
The bitterness of yesterday is gone.
The memories of your life remain.
Today, I choose to wait, to love
In my heart and in my mind.
Today, I choose to feel joy
Because you are a part of my journey.
You will remain in my heart forever.
We need each other—come back to me.

# *Love*

What is love, and where is it found?
Is it found in your smile and in your touch?
Is it found in the silence of your words?
In the twinkle of your eyes,
Love is the watchful eye of a mother,
The curious eyes of a child.
Love is true without conditions.
Truth in love is what we seek.
What is your truth?
God is love; my heart belongs to Him.
Come, let us share His love.

# What Is Life?

Life is about living.
Life has a beginning and an end.
It is up to you to learn to live,
Appreciating all the colors of the rainbow,
Sinking into all the joys,
Saturating yourself with sunshine,
Wading through the highs and lows,
Gliding when things get tough.
Wading during the murky times,
What happens when you cannot talk,
Unable to talk, sealed in unspoken words,
Hiding behind unspoken words,
Afraid of talking because the words
May come out and be hurtful?
What happens when you do not walk?
Fear takes over, afraid of falling.
Accept the hand extended in love.
When you can hold someone's hand,
There is trust in your heart.
Hold a hand whenever you can.
Rejoice in your heart that you are alive,
Feeling life-giving love and touching
The hand that reaches out to you.

# *Discovery*

*Racing through the years of life,*
*Lost in time between tasks,*
*Going through the motions*
*On the edge of discovery,*
*Today is a new day for reaching*
*Deep inside and finding strength,*
*Tackling the present, being strong,*
*Putting the past in its place,*
*Moving forward each new day,*
*Facing the mystery of the present.*
*Time to take a chance and live—*
*No more racing through the years,*
*Moving with deliberate intentions,*
*Exploring a new path with strength,*
*Choosing joy and peace.*
*This is a new day to*
*Discover how it feels to be whole.*

# The Eyes of a Child

Through the eyes of a child,
At the end of the rainbow is a pot of gold;
My grandson told me so.
Look through your childish eyes,
And turn to your mother.
You will see that she is the rainbow.
Her heart is the pot of gold
Holding joy, love, dreams, and hope.
You will need these for a lifetime—
The joy in life she will share with you,
The love she will always give to you,
The hope that you will be successful,
Navigating the journey of your own life.
And she holds dreams of grandeur
That all your dreams come true.
The rainbow of all the colors of life,
The bright and vibrant colors of life,
Your pot of gold is the love in her heart—
Is yours to share until forever.
Your mother is your rainbow.

# *Move On*

*Move on—stop your waiting.*
*Stop worrying and wondering—move on.*
*Embrace the life you have.*
*Savor the beautiful memories.*
*Say, "I have two beautiful, sweet grandsons."*
*They are not with you, so remember—*
*Remember when they once were, and smile.*
*It is time to stop crying; dry your tears.*
*They are not here, but they love you.*
*Love does not die. Hope does not die.*
*Do not carry this burden anymore.*
*If it is meant to be, one day, they will come.*
*It may not be when you want them to come.*
*Love will lead them, and they will come.*
*God will create a special season so they*
*Will come to you, the grandmother they miss.*
*Your beautiful daughter you cherish even today*
*Is slowly finding her way back to you.*
*Allow yourself to trust she is taking the road*
*Traveled by many—that bumpy, winding road*
*That keeps a person lost and confused.*
*She has not forgotten how much you love her.*
*The road she is on is really rough.*
*Stop wondering and worrying;*
*She is on her own life's journey, and*
*Only God knows when she will be strong enough to come back*
*To you, who, through Him, gave her life. Move on.*

# P Is for Power

The P words hold power.
They can rule, or you can rule.
Consider how powerful pain is.
Pain has the power to kill.
Dwelling on pain of the past can kill.
The P words embody the power to kill
Only if you allow them to take control.
This is the season for you to have power.
The power is within you to take control.
Take control of the pain, and you can kill it.
You can rid yourself of pain you carry from the past.
Take charge of all the P words, and when you do,
You will find the most powerful P words that exist.
The most powerful P words are prayer and peace.
You can stop the madness in your life through prayer.
You can find joy again with the peace that prayer brings.
Pray, and peace will come. Now hear me, please,
And use your God-given power for prayer and peace.
Peace is here; you must believe and know you have power.
Seek, and you will find peace—the door will open.
The Peacemaker wants us all to live in peace.

# God Is Watching over You

God is watching over you every day.
In the quiet hours of the morning, He is there.
He is watching when you are confused and feeling lost.
When you are trying to escape the loneliness
And feel you do not want to go on,
He knows how tired you are, and He feeds you.
He gives you just enough fuel to get you through the day.
The pain is great; your burden seems too heavy to bear.
Yet, He is watching the healing process, the small steps.
You don't even realize that He is there, holding you
In the palms of His hands, taking care of His piece of clay.
You rest your head on His shoulders. You know He is with you.
He is there as you slowly come alive; He provides.
His angels are with you every day, gently guiding you.
He knows you will be whole again, not pretending but really living.
He provides just enough love—the precious fuel of life—
To keep you going, pressing on, holding on to each day.
Because you are loved, you know you must not give up.
You are here in God's country, in the healing mountains,
The hills from whence cometh your help. These mountains
He has given you to love, to live, and grow in; you do love them.
You will stay strong because it is His will—He is breathing
The breath of life into you every day, watching you grow stronger.
Go ahead; reach out, and take His hand. God is with you,
   God is guiding you, God is helping you, and God is watching over you.

# *More or Less*

Less is better; I'll take a little of this and a little of that.
Just a little is just enough.
I have stepped up on this grand stage.
I am a senior in every way.
Proud to be a senior,
I have been over the hill and up the mountain.
As I stand on this stage, I know less is better.
A little less of anything makes me happy—
Less sugar, less stuff, less time,
Less tension, less discussion.
Whatever it is, I require less.
Is there anything to want more of?
The answer is yes—
More love, more laughs, more smiles,
More joy. This is my time for joy.
Now a super senior, I have graduated from various schools.
I have learned less is better.
Lighten you load; get rid of More, and embrace Less.

# The Journey

*Where does this journey in life take you?*
*I feel I am getting sicker and sicker.*
*My pain is not visible.*
*My symptoms are not visible;*
*Neither is my fear.*
*What can I do?*
*I can reshape my life.*
*I can take my life back.*
*I can give myself the things I need.*
*I can block the energy suckers.*
*I know I can change.*
*I can hold on to the change I seek.*
*I can find my voice—*
*The voice that is silent when it should be heard.*
*I can find the strength I need—*
*The strength that has brought me where I am now.*
*I will get rid of anger and replace it with joy.*
*I will stand tall and take responsibility for myself.*
*I can love me better.*
*I can get the help I need.*
*I can do what is necessary to take care of myself.*
*I can find joy in the simplicity of life.*
*I will cast away fear and embrace joy.*
*I can take a stand and stand my ground.*

# *Dreaming*

I see you standing there.
If I say I don't want to go on, what would you do?
If I speak of the pain I feel, what would you do?
When life is not easy, what do you say?
I look at you and say, "Come home."
As I awaken, thoughts flood
Through my head
Like a whirling wind lingering daily.
I pray the storm will go away.
I fall asleep and dream
Of the day you return to me
If only in my dream.

# Silence

Silence is not golden.
Where there is silence, there is pain.
Silence fills an empty space.
Anyone can be wrapped up in silence.
At first, you think it is a cozy place.
Then you know full well the
Pain caused by nonexpression.
By not saying what you feel,
You become locked in silence.
You begin to wonder where your voice is.
Silence happens in avoidance.
It may be that you choose not to respond in haste
Or simply do not know what to say.
Are you afraid to speak your mind?
You know words have power,
And you keep your words to yourself.
You keep them tight inside, protecting
The person you want to be—A Godly person,
A peacekeeper, a guardian, a thoughtful and caring person.
Silence has been with you so long
You don't know what to do with it.
Yes, you know what has happened.
Eyes wide open, you now want to change.
You want to speak out and shout,
Yet you find yourself locked in your silence.
Silence is not golden.
Silence keeps you in a dark place.

# The Box

There is a box.
Does it belong to me?
The box is empty,
And so is she—
Without legs,
Without desire,
Without plans.
Tired of living in that box,
She chooses to break free.
There is a box.

# A Puzzle

There is a puzzle in front of you,
A new and seemingly easy puzzle.
This puzzle is not easy;
The parts have been shaped
Over the years by pain,
Heartache, fear, and experience.
You are charged with putting
This puzzle back together.
You find that the pieces you see
Don't fit together easily.
The head is not working,
The heart is broken,
The hands are all over the place,
And the health is a real mess.
You start with the head and
Think the heart is more important.
Then back and forth you go from
Head to heart to hands and health.
One day, the lights come on, and
You find the formula in the head
That makes assembly manageable—
Head, heart, health, and hands.
Working with the head and heart brings
Understanding and togetherness.
You complete this whole person puzzle.

# Whom Do You See?

*Whom do you see when you look at me?*
*Do you see whom I see?*
*The person you see is Invisible Me.*
*I do not want you to see the person I see.*
*The person you see is not really me.*
*Whom do I see when I look at me?*
*A person full of doubts and fears,*
*Many fears about life and love,*
*A person hiding within her mind,*
*Not wishing to share who is really inside.*
*A person full of desire for more—*
*More love, more life,*
*More peace, more joy—*
*That is the person I see.*
*Whom do you see when you look at me?*

# Why Eagles Fly

I am standing here watching an eagle fly,
This majestic bird gliding across the sky,
This big and powerful bird holding my gaze
As she dips and dives all over the place
Searching, soaring, looking all around,
Trying to find her place on the ground—
Her sacred place where she can work
To care for herself and her family,
Another place where she can hide,
Where she feels safe from the world outside.
Her eyes wide open and wings outstretched,
She reaches and turns, doing her best.
Why is she soaring and flying high?
She has to survive, and that is why
This eagle that caught my eye does not
Wear a smile high up in the sky.
This majestic creature of habit is she,
Instinctively flying and entertaining me,
Repeating her fight day after day.
She flies because that is what she knows.
Saving herself from a watchful eye,
Knowing someone watches every move,
She knows, and she flies to get away,
Saving her life, flying high in the sky,
Escaping the gaze of those nearby.

# *I Chose to Live*

*When my days were dark and dreary, I chose to live.*
*When my eyes wanted to shed tears, I chose to live.*
*I chose to live through the pain.*
*I chose to live through the heartache.*
*When the news was not what I expected, I chose to live.*
*At times when I felt at the end of my rope, I chose.*
*The clock kept ticking; I chose the music.*
*My heart kept beating, and I danced.*
*When everyone around me said to rest,*
*I chose to live—I ran to the joy in this life.*
*I ran to loving arms for their embrace.*
*I knew I could not stop choosing the road less traveled.*
*I knew I had to chase the rainbow; I sang.*
*I smiled in spite of the fear, the news that things*
*Were not going in the right direction, that my tests*
*Were not indicating a reason to keep the faith.*
*I chose—I chose to have faith that this was my day to live.*
*I chose to live; God granted me the right to choose.*
*I heard His whispers in my ear to choose, saying,*
*"Do not choose fear; do not choose doubt; choose to believe*
*With every breath in your body—choose to live."*
*He whispered, "When the time comes—and it will be My time to choose—*
*Then and only then will I choose you and say,*
*'Well done, My good and faithful servant.*
*You have already chosen Me.'"*

# Music from Your Heart

*In the quiet of the evening as*
*I sit near to you,*
*I hear the songs coming from your heart—*
*The songs of joy and happiness,*
*The songs of peace,*
*The songs of contentment,*
*Soothing songs that touch me*
*In secret places hidden deep inside*
*The sacred places of joy and peace.*
*The words move and speak to me*
*Of the love that is shared between us,*
*Words of power and surrender.*
*I love this music that comes from your heart—*
*This sweet silence that resonates so loud.*
*Yes, keep this music coming from your heart.*
*Sing to me; sing to me more and more.*
*Let this music from your heart continue*
*To flow from you to me, and I will return*
*To you the love I feel in this music from your soul.*

# Rain

His love is like the rain. Oh, I feel the joy of the rain.
The coolness surrounds me, and it feels so good.
Why do I run for cover? I run to escape.
I must get away. Shelter? Not the shelter of his arms.
To feel the warmth of his body, I cannot go there.
I can imagine just how nice it would be temporarily.
How nice it would be, but only temporarily.
When the rain stops and the sun shines, again his love will leave,
And I will lose the joy of his love.
His love will leave with the rain.
His love is like the rain, occasional. I will only feel his love
Occasionally. I do love rainy days. Only when it rains can I feel
His love. That is not good enough for me. Or … is it? … Is it?
Is it the rain that I need to replenish me—like the plants of this earth?
Oh rain, then you must come to me. Replenish me so I can go on.
Refresh me. Drench me with your soul. Love me,
Even if it's for a short while—his love is like the rain.
I need it to replenish me. Let it rain.

# The Walk

*I will take a walk in the woods and bare my soul to you.*
*The trees will keep all our secrets.*
*There is joy in memories of the past.*
*Come to me;*
*Let us rejoice in the present together.*
*Forgiveness brings clarity*
*And lifts you to experience higher heights in all that you do.*
*Hold my hand.*
*Let us find forgiveness together;*
*Let's walk in the woods and bear our souls together.*
*The trees will keep all our secrets.*
*With age comes wisdom.*
*When your day of wisdom and reckoning arrives,*
*You will realize the treasures your youth threw away.*
*Running out of time is where I am today.*
*Out of time is where you will be in your tomorrow.*
*Tomorrow is the day I wait for your return.*
*Many tomorrows have come and gone.*
*Still I wait.*
*Is it possible to rejoice in tomorrow?*
*Today is the tomorrow I have been waiting for.*
*I will use it wisely and rejoice in it today.*

Printed in the United States
By Bookmasters